BECOMING A CITIZEN

A TRUE BOOK

by
Sarah De Capua

ϘϷ

Children's Press®
A Division of Scholastic Inc.

New York Toronto London Auckland Sydney
Mexico City New Delhi Hong Kong
Danbury, Connecticut

A new U.S. citizen proudly holds his Certificate of Naturalization.

Reading Consultant
Nanci R. Vargus, Ed.D.
*Teacher in Residence
University of Indianapolis
Indianapolis, Indiana*

*Dedication:
To Christopher*

The photograph on the cover shows Chinese immigrants studying English. The photograph on the title page shows a mother and her adopted daughter celebrating after the daughter's U.S. citizenship ceremony.

Library of Congress Cataloging-in-Publication Data

De Capua, Sarah.
    Becoming a citizen / Sarah De Capua.
        p. cm.
    Includes bibliographical references and index.
    ISBN 0-516-22331-3 (lib.bdg.)   0-516-27366-3 (pbk.)
    1. Citizenship—United States—Juvenile literature. 2. Naturalization—
United States—Juvenile literature. [1. Citizenship. 2. Naturalization.]
I. Title. II. Series.

KF4700.Z9 D4 2002
342.73'083—dc21   2001017184

Contents

Immigrants taking an oath of allegiance to the United States during their citizenship ceremony

What Is a Citizen?

A citizen is a member of a particular country. Citizens have the right to live in their country permanently and are protected by its government.

Anyone who was born in the United States is a citizen of the United States. Many people have come to the

European immigrants arriving in the United States in the 1920s

United States from other countries to live permanently. These people are called immigrants.

There are two kinds of immigrants—legal and illegal.

Legal immigrants have permission from the U.S. government to enter the country. Illegal immigrants do not have permission to live in the United States, and cannot become

Legal immigrants have permission to enter the United States.

citizens. They are breaking the law and can be sent back to their home country.

Legal immigrants are welcome to become U.S. citizens. As citizens, they may enjoy all the rights and responsibilities that come with being a citizen.

United States citizens have many rights. These include:

- the right to vote in local, state, and national elections

- the right to run for public office (Immigrants who become

The many rights of U.S. citizens include the right to run for public office (above) and the right to vote (right).

U.S. citizens may run for any public office except for U.S. president or vice president. A person must be born in the United States to qualify for those positions.)

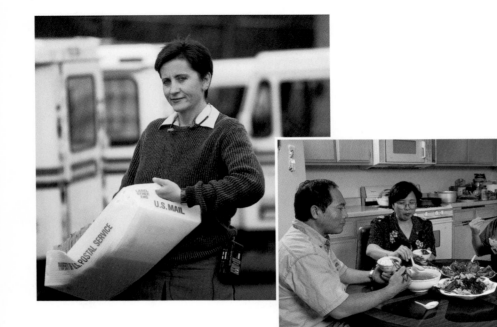

U.S. citizens also enjoy the right to seek a government job (left) and bring other family members to the United States (right).

• the right to seek a government job

• the right to bring other family members to the United States legally

- the right to live in the United States permanently

Along with the rights of citizenship come many responsibilities. Good citizens:

- stay informed about important issues so that they can choose leaders wisely

- get involved in their local community

- register to vote

- obey U.S. laws

- pay taxes

Responsible citizens get involved in their local community (top), register to vote (left), and serve on a jury when chosen (opposite).

- serve on a jury when chosen

- serve in the armed forces when required

Becoming a citizen involves
several steps. It may take many
months to complete all the
steps. But with hard work,
study, and honesty, it is not too
difficult to become a citizen.

Green Cards

PERMANENT RESIDENT CARD

NAME SMITH, JOHN Q.

INS A# 963-796-776

Birthdate   Category
10/04/49   P26

Sex
M

Country of Birth
Canada

CARD EXPIRES 11/01/94

Resident Since 11/01/97

C1USA9730050225EAC9730050225<<
4910040M9411014CAN<<<<<<<<<<<8
SMITH<<<<<< JOHN <Q<<<<<<<<<<<<

Permanent legal immigrants carry identification cards. This card proves that the immigrant has permission to live and work in the United States. The card includes the person's name, date of birth, photograph, and fingerprint. These cards may be almost any color, but are usually called "green cards."

Who Can Become a Citizen?

Naturalization (NACH-ur-uhl-i-ZAY-shun) is the process of becoming a U.S. citizen. The U.S. Congress has passed laws that govern the rules immigrants must follow to become U.S. citizens. The rules are the same for all

A woman reading a guide on how to become a U.S. citizen

men and women, no matter what country they come from.

Before the naturalization process can begin, immigrants must meet several requirements. Among the requirements are:

• Immigrants must be at least 18 years old. However, a child can be naturalized if an adult submits an application for him or her.

• Immigrants must have a green card to prove they are living in the United States legally.

• In most cases, immigrants must have been permanent residents of the United States for at least 5 years.

• Immigrants must have good moral character. This means

After living and working in the United States for a number of years, some immigrants decide to become U.S. citizens.

they must not abuse alcohol or drugs, sell drugs, or lie in order to become U.S. citizens. Also, they must not be members of any anti-U.S.-government group.

• Immigrants must not have broken any U.S. immigration laws.

• Immigrants should be able to understand, speak, read, and write simple English in order to pass the citizenship test. Exceptions may be made for people with mental disabilities or elderly people who have

Immigrants studying English

lived in the United States for many years. They may be allowed to take the test in their own language or take a simpler test.

• Immigrants must be willing to take an oath pledging to be loyal to the United States, to obey the laws of the United States, and to serve in the armed forces if needed.

Once immigrants meet these requirements, they are ready to begin the naturalization process.

Applying for Naturalization

The Application for Naturalization is known as Form N-400. This is the form that most immigrants who want to become citizens complete. However, there are different forms depending on an immigrant's personal circumstances. For example, different forms are required for

A Guatemalan family learning about applying for naturalization

foreign-born children of naturalized citizens and for children adopted from other countries.

American parents who adopt children from other countries can submit naturalization applications for their children.

When complete, Form N-400 is sent to the Immigration and Naturalization Service (INS). The INS is the government agency that keeps track of immigration. The INS also grants citizenship to people who want to become naturalized.

Immigrants can call, visit, or write to their nearest INS office for application forms. There are four main INS offices in the

People picking up application forms at an INS office in Los Angeles

United States. They are located in Nebraska, California, Texas, and Vermont. Application forms are also available on the Internet.

Form N-400 has about twelve parts. It asks for basic information, such as the person's name and address. It also asks for information about the person's employment and whether he or she has ever broken the law.

An applicant should use a typewriter or print neatly when

Most immigrants applying for U.S. citizenship must complete Form N-400.

completing the form. All questions must be answered honestly and completely.

Along with Form N-400, two photographs of the applicant must be included, as well as a photocopy of the applicant's green card and a check for $250. The check covers the application fee as well as a fingerprinting fee. The applicant's fingerprints are taken later in the naturalization process.

An applicant must be careful to include all the required materials when returning Form N-400 to the INS. Forgetting to

A woman mailing her application form to the INS

include two photographs, a copy of the applicant's green card, or a check for $250 will delay the application process.

The Citizenship Test

After the application for citizenship is mailed to the INS, there is usually a long wait. The wait may be as long as one year. Applicants use this time to learn about U.S. history and government. They will need this information in order to pass the

Immigrants taking a class to prepare for the citizenship test

citizenship test. If necessary, they should also study English.

Every person who wants to become a naturalized U.S. citizen must take this test. Many communities offer citizenship classes to help people prepare for it. Most local libraries have citizenship-test workbooks, which people study before they take the test.

During the waiting period, the INS contacts applicants to inform them where and when to have their fingerprints taken. The fingerprints are then sent to the INS. Finally, the INS is ready to test and interview the applicant. The INS sends a letter to inform the applicant when the citizenship test will take place.

During the test, an INS official asks the applicant questions about U.S. government and history. The questions are asked in English.

The applicant must answer them in English.

There are one hundred possible questions that an applicant must know the answers to in order to pass the test. About

A man studies the list of possible questions that could be asked during the citizenship test.

twenty of these questions are asked during the test. At least twelve of them must be answered correctly.

During the interview, applicants must take an oath, or make a promise, to tell the truth. Then they must answer questions about their N-400 application, their work, and their families. It is important to tell the truth throughout the naturalization process. Anyone who answers a question dishonestly can be denied citizenship.

The applicant finds out right away if he or she has passed the test and interview. If the applicant does not pass, he or she can try again. If the applicant does pass, there is just one more step to becoming a citizen.

Could You Pass the

Here are a few questions that could be asked on the citizenship test. Do you know the answers?

1. Can you name the thirteen original states?

2. What is the date of Independence Day?

3. How many states are there in the Union?

4. Where is the nation's capital located?

5. When and where was the Declaration of Independence adopted?

An Independence Day celebration in New York City

Citizenship Test?

The signing of the Declaration of Independence

Answers: 1. Connecticut, Delaware, Georgia, Maryland, Massachusetts, New Hampshire, New Jersey, New York, North Carolina, Pennsylvania, Rhode Island, South Carolina, and Virginia; 2. July 4; 3. fifty; 4. Washington, D.C.; 5. July 4, 1776, in Philadelphia, Pennsylvania.

The Citizenship Ceremony

The brief citizenship ceremony is the most important step in the naturalization process. It marks the moment when a person officially becomes a naturalized U.S. citizen.

Several months after passing the citizenship test, the

A huge citizenship ceremony in Miami, Florida

person receives a letter from the INS. This letter states when and where the ceremony will take place. Some ceremonies are held in courtrooms. Sometimes large groups of people are ready to be naturalized at the same time. Then the ceremony takes place in an auditorium or theater.

At the ceremony, each applicant must take an oath of allegiance, or loyalty, to

Parents taking the oath of allegiance during the citizenship ceremony for their adopted baby girl

the United States. The person swears to be loyal to the United States and to obey its laws. The person also promises to fight in the U.S. armed forces if needed. Finally, the person must swear that he or she wants to become a United States citizen.

After the oath has been taken, each new citizen receives a Certificate of Naturalization. This official document shows that the person is a citizen of the United States. For many people, the day they become U.S. citizens is remembered as one of the most important days in their lives.

Proud parents hold up their son's Certificate of Naturalization (above), and a new American citizen hugs a friend (right).

To Find Out More

Here are some additional resources to help you learn more about immigration and citizenship:

 **Books**

Bratman, Fred, and Samuel D. Woods. **Becoming a Citizen: Adopting a New Home.** Raintree Steck-Vaughn, 1993.

De Capua, Sarah. **Running for Public Office.** Children's Press, 2002.

De Capua, Sarah. **Serving on a Jury.** Children's Press, 2002.

De Capua, Sarah. **Voting.** Children's Press, 2002.

Freedman, Russell. **Immigrant Kids.** Puffin, 1995.

Organizations and Online Sites

American Immigration Center

http://www.us-immigration.com

This site offers informative materials about immigration, naturalization, becoming a citizen, and more. Includes a tutorial that explains the basics of immigration.

Immigration and Naturalization Service

http://www.ins.usdoj.gov

Features naturalization requirements, fingerprint procedures, and application forms. Includes FAQs, general information, and links to related sites.

National Citizenship Network

http://www.irsa-uscr.org

This site includes updated information and statistics about immigration and U.S. citizenship.

Study for the Citizenship Test

http://www.uscitizenship.org

Take a look at the U.S. citizenship test and find out how much you already know—or need to learn—about the United States. Includes links to other sites.

Important Words

applicant someone who is applying for something, such as a job

armed forces all of the branches of a country's military

ceremony formal actions, words, or music performed to mark an important occasion

foreign coming from another country

jury group of people at a trial who listen to the facts and decide whether the person accused of a crime is guilty or not guilty

mental disabilities problems with a person's brain that make it harder to do some things other people can do

petition written request

right something that the law says you can have or do, as in the right to vote

46

Index

Meet the Author

Sarah De Capua received her master of arts in teaching in 1993 and has since been educating children, first as a teacher and currently as an editor and author of children's books. Other books she has written for Children's Press include: *Paying Taxes, Running for Public Office, Serving on a Jury, Voting* (True Books); *J.C. Watts, Jr.: Character Counts* (Community Builders); and several titles in the Rookie-Read-About® geography series.

Ms. De Capua resides in Colorado.